Camping Out

by William Overturf
illustrated by Carol Heyer

Core Decodable 113

Plans for a Camp Out........................3
Afraid in the Tent..............................10

McGraw Hill Education

Bothell, WA • Chicago, IL • Columbus, OH • New York, NY

MHEonline.com

Send all inquiries to:
McGraw-Hill Education
8787 Orion Place
Columbus, OH 43240

ISBN: 978-0-02-140694-4
MHID: 0-02-140694-4

Printed in Canada.

9 10 11 12 KOD 24

Plans for a Camp Out

The girls waited all week. On Saturday, they would camp out. They would sleep on the ground in a tent.

"I hope I will not be afraid," said Brook. "I have never camped before."

"We will be right in town," said Audrey.

"And we will be next to my house. My mom and dad will be around," Audrey added. "You will enjoy camping out."

At last, it was Saturday night. Audrey's dad made dinner. He grilled corn in foil. He also made sweet and sour chicken.

At nine, there were no clouds in the dark sky. The girls saw the round moon and a thousand stars.

Audrey's mom and dad said good night. The girls crawled in the tent.

"Are you afraid, Brook?" asked Audrey.

Brook thought about it. She was surprised. She did not feel afraid.

"Wow," said Brook. "I feel fine now."

Afraid in the Tent

Brook quickly fell asleep. Audrey did not. She felt afraid!

"Being afraid is stupid," she thought. "I am right by my house."

Audrey heard a loud sound. Was it a growl? There was more noise. Was an animal prowling around?

Brook just slept.

Audrey felt very afraid. What could she do? Call her mom? Run to the house?

"I must stay," she frowned.

Then Audrey heard a loud howl! She jumped. Her hand felt the cold, moist soil. There might be bugs in the ground!

Audrey slid down in her sleeping bag. She felt so afraid. She did not even have the power to talk.

Audrey was awake for a long, long time. She thought she heard a mouse. She thought she heard a shout.

And Brook just slept.

The sun woke Brook up. "I slept well," she said.

Audrey did not say a thing. She was sound asleep at last.